The Juicing and Smoothie Ultimate Recipe Book

The Complete Guide to Healthy Juices & Smoothies
Easy recipes for Weight Loss & Cleanses
Suitable for the Nutribullet, Nutri Ninja and Vitamix

Hannah A. Johnson

Copyright Legal Information

Table of Contents

Mangoes Everywhere 38

Vegetable Your Life 44

Milkshake The Smoothie Life 70

The Tea Haven 78

Introduction

NUTRI NINJA is a juicer and blender that can be used to extract juices from both fruits and vegetables.

As you know, it is important to incorporate these in your diet as much as possible in order to achieve good health.

This book provides you with simple recipes that you can try and enhance and practice good health.

Thank you again for purchasing this book and I hope you find it interesting and helpful in pursuing your healthy lifestyle.

Let us begin!

Berrielicious
Just for You

BERRY LEMON SMOOTHIE

INGREDIENTS:

- 1 cup blueberries, chopped
- 1 cup strawberries, chopped
- 1 cup blackberries, chopped
- 1 cup lemon juice
- 1/2 cups plain yogurt
- ½ teaspoon salt
- 2 tablespoons sugar
- Mint leaves
- Ice cubes

RECIPE:

1. Add the blueberries, strawberries, blackberries, lemon and yogurt to a blender and whizz until smooth.
2. Add in the salt and sugar and blend until well combined.
3. Add the ice cubes and blend.
4. Serve cold with a sprinkling of fresh mint leaves.

BERRY AND OATMEAL MILKSHAKE

INGREDIENTS:

- 1 cup regular oatmeal
- 1 cup strawberries, chopped
- 1 cup blueberries chopped
- 1 cup full cream milk
- 1 large banana, chopped
- 2 tablespoons sugar
- Mint leaves
- Ice cubes

RECIPE:

1. Add the oatmeal to a blender along with the strawberries and blueberries and whizz until smooth.
2. Add in the cream and banana and blend.
3. Add the sugar and ice cubes and whizz until well combined.
4. Serve cold with a sprinkling of mint leaves on top.

RASPBERRY PINEAPPLE MINT JUICE

INGREDIENTS:

- 1 cup pineapple, chopped
- 1 cup raspberries, chopped
- 1 cup lemon juice
- ½ teaspoon salt
- 1 tablespoon honey
- 1 cup mint leaves
- Ice cubes

RECIPE:

1. Add the pineapple to the juicer and extract the juice.
2. Add the raspberries to the juicer and extract the juice.
3. Add the two to a pitcher and mix until well combined.
4. Add in the lemon juice and mix well.
5. Add in salt and honey and mix until well combined.
6. Add in the mint leaves and use a muddler to crush it gently.
7. Add the ice cubes and mix.
8. Serve cold.

RASPBERRY GRAPE JUICE

INGREDIENTS:

- 1 cup grapes, chopped
- 1 cup raspberries, chopped
- 1 cup lemon juice
- ½ teaspoon salt
- 1 tablespoon honey
- Mint leaves
- Ice cubes

RECIPE:

1. Add the grapes to the juicer and extract the juice.
2. Add the raspberries to the juice and extract the juice.
3. Combine the two in a pitcher and mix.
4. Add in the lemon juice and mix until well combined.
5. Toss in the salt and stir.
6. Add in the honey and mix until well combined.
7. Add in chopped mint leaves and ice cubes and mix.
8. Serve cold.

RASPBERRY LYCHEE MINT JUICE

INGREDIENTS:

- 1 cup lychees, chopped
- 1 cup raspberries, chopped
- 1 cup orange juice
- ½ teaspoon salt
- 1 tablespoon honey
- 1 cup mint leaves
- Ice cubes

RECIPE:

1. Add the lychees to the juicer and extract the juice.
2. Add the raspberries to the juicer and extract the juice.
3. Add the two to the pitcher and mix until well combined.
4. Add in the orange juice and mix well.
5. Add the salt, and honey and mix until well combined.
6. Add the mint leaves and use a muddler to extract the flavor.
7. Add in ice cubes and mix well.
8. Serve cold.

BLACKBERRY AND ORANGE JUICE

INGREDIENTS:

- 1 cup blackberries, chopped
- 1 cup oranges, chopped
- 1 cup lemon juice
- ½ teaspoon salt
- 1 tablespoon honey
- Mint leaves
- Ice cubes

RECIPE:

1. Add the blackberries to a juicer and extract the juice.
2. Add the oranges to a juicer and extract the juice.
3. Add the two to a pitcher and add in the lemon juice.
4. Mix and toss in the salt.
5. Add in the honey and mint leaves and use a muddler to crush the mint leaves.
6. Add in the ice cubes and stir.
7. Serve cold.

BLUEBERRY SMOOTHIE

INGREDIENTS:

- 2 cups blueberries, chopped
- 1 cup banana, chopped
- 2 cups plain yogurt
- ½ teaspoon salt
- 2 tablespoons honey
- Mint leaves
- Ice cubes

RECIPE:

1. Add the blueberries to a blender along with the banana and yogurt and whizz until smooth.
2. Add in the salt and honey and whizz further.
3. Add in the ice cubes and whizz further.
4. Serve with a sprinkling of mint leaves.

BLUEBERRIES AND ORANGE

INGREDIENTS:

- 1 cup oranges, chopped
- 1 cup blueberries, chopped
- 1 cup orange juice
- ½ teaspoon salt
- 1 tablespoon honey
- Mint leaves
- Ice cubes

RECIPE:

1. Add the oranges to a juicer and extract the juice.
2. Add the blueberries to the juicer and extract the juice.
3. Combine the two in a pitcher and well combine.
4. Add in the orange juice and mix until well combined.
5. Add the salt, honey and chopped mint leaves and use a muddler to crush the mint.
6. Add in ice cubes and stir.
7. Serve cold.

STRAWBERRY AND MANGO PUNCH

INGREDIENTS:

- 1 cup strawberry, chopped
- 1 cup mangoes, chopped
- 1 cup orange juice
- ½ teaspoon salt
- 1 tablespoon honey
- Mint leaves
- Ice cubes

RECIPE:

1. Add the strawberries to a juicer and extract the juice.
2. Add the mangoes to the blender and make a pulp.
3. Combine the two in a pitcher.
4. Add in the orange juice and mix until well combined.
5. Add the salt and honey and mix until well combined.
6. Add the mint leaves and use a muddler to extract the flavor.
7. Add in the ice cubes and mix well.
8. Serve cold.

STRAWBERRY AND PINEAPPLE JUICE

INGREDIENTS:

- 1 cup strawberries, chopped
- 1 cup pineapple, chopped
- 1 cup lemon juice
- ½ teaspoon salt
- 1 tablespoon honey
- Mint leaves
- Ice cubes

RECIPE:

1. Add the strawberry to the blender and whizz until smooth.
2. Add the pineapple to the juicer and extract the juice.
3. Add the two to a pitcher along with the lemon juice and mix until well combined.
4. Add in the salt and mix until well combined.
5. Add the honey and use a muddler to mix.
6. Add the mint leaves and ice cubes and use a muddler to crush the leaves.
7. Serve cold.

STRAWBERRY KIWI MILKSHAKE

INGREDIENTS:

- 1 cup kiwi, chopped
- 1 cup strawberry, chopped
- 2 cups coconut milk
- ½ teaspoon salt
- Mint leaves, chopped
- Ice cubes

RECIPE:

1. Add the kiwi to a blender along with half the coconut milk and whizz.
2. Add to a pitcher.
3. Add the strawberry to a blender along with the coconut milk and whizz.
4. Add both to a pitcher and add in the salt.
5. Mix until well combined.
6. Add in the ice cubes and mix.
7. Serve cold with a sprinkling of mint leaves.

STRAWBERRY CHOCOLATE MILKSHAKE

INGREDIENTS:

- 2 cups strawberry, chopped
- 1 cup chocolate, chopped
- 2 cups coconut milk
- ½ teaspoon salt
- Mint leaves
- Ice cubes

RECIPE:

1. Add the strawberry and coconut milk to a blender and whizz until smooth.
2. Toss in the chocolate and mix until well combined.
3. Add to a glass and mix in salt.
4. Add the ice cubes and stir until well combined.
5. Serve with a sprinkling of mint leaves.

CHERRY GREEN TEA JUICE

INGREDIENTS:

- 1 cup cherries, chopped
- 1 cup hot water, chopped
- 1 green tea bag
- 1 cup lemon juice
- 1 tablespoon honey
- Mint leaves
- Ice cubes

RECIPE:

1. Add the cherries to the juicer and extract the juice.
2. Add the tea bag to a cup and add in the hot water.
3. Allow the tea bag to release flavor.
4. Meanwhile, add the cherry juice to a pitcher and add in the lemon juice.
5. Mix well and add in the tea.
6. Add honey and mix until well combined.
7. Add in mint leaves and use a muddler to crush.
8. Add ice cubes and stir.
9. Serve cold.

CHERRY SMOOTHIE

INGREDIENTS:

- 1 cups cherries, chopped
- 1 large banana, chopped
- 2 cups milk
- 2 tablespoons honey
- Ice cubes

RECIPE:

1. Add the cherries to a blender along with the banana and milk and whizz until smooth.
2. Add in the honey and ice and whizz until smooth.
3. Add to a glass and serve cold.

CRANBERRY AND LEMON JUICE

INGREDIENTS:

- 1 cup cranberries, chopped
- 1 cup strawberries, chopped
- 1 cup lemon juice
- ½ teaspoon salt
- 1 tablespoon honey
- Mint leaves
- Ice cubes

RECIPE:

1. Add the cranberries to a juicer and extract the juice.
2. Add the strawberries and juice.
3. Add the two to a pitcher along with the lemon juice and mix until well combined.
4. Add in the salt and honey and mix well.
5. Add the mint leaves and combine.
6. Add ice cubes and stir.
7. Serve cold.

CRANBERRY SMOOTHIE

INGREDIENTS:

- 2 cups cranberries, chopped
- 1 cup almond milk
- 1 cups coconut milk
- ½ teaspoon salt
- 2 tablespoons honey
- Mint leaves
- Ice cubes

RECIPE:

1. Add the cranberries to a blender along with the almond milk and yogurt and whizz until smooth.
2. Add in the salt and honey and whizz.
3. Add in the ice cubes and whizz.
4. Serve with a sprinkling of mint leaves on top.

Apple
Everything

APPLE PEAR JUICE

INGREDIENTS:

- 1 cup pear, chopped
- 1 cup apples, chopped
- 1 cup orange juice
- ½ teaspoon salt
- 1 tablespoon honey
- Mint leaves
- Ice cubes

RECIPE:

1. Add the pear to a juicer and extract the juice.
2. Add the apples to a juicer and extract the juice.
3. Combine the two in a pitcher along with the orange juice and mix until well combined.
4. Add in the salt and honey and mix.
5. Add in the mint leaves and use a muddler to extract the flavor.
6. Add in ice cubes and mix.
7. Serve cold.

APPLE APRICOT JUICE

INGREDIENTS:

- 1 cup apples, chopped
- 1 cup apricots chopped
- 1 cup orange juice
- 1 lemon, juiced
- Mint leaves
- Ice cubes

RECIPE:

1. Add the apples to the juicer and extract the juice.
2. Add the apricots to the juicer and extract the juice.
3. Add them to a pitcher along with the orange juice and mix until well combined.
4. Squeeze in the lemon juice and mix.
5. Chop the mint leaves and add to the pitcher.
6. Add in the ice cubes and mix until well combined.
7. Serve cold.

Apple Berry Juice

INGREDIENTS:

- 1 cup frozen mixed berries
- 1 cup apples, chopped
- 1 cup pears, chopped
- ½ teaspoon salt
- 1 tablespoon honey
- Mint leaves
- Ice cubes

RECIPE:

1. Add the apples to a juicer and extract the juice.
2. Add the fresh apple juice to a blender along with frozen berries and chopped pears, blend until mixed.
3. Pour into a pitcher stir in the salt and honey and mint leaves. Add in ice cubes and mix well. Serve cold or keep refrigerated.

Apple Sparkling Grape Juice

INGREDIENTS:

- 1 cup apples, chopped
- 3 cups green grapes
- 1 cup orange juice
- 1 cup sparkling water
- 1 lemon, juiced
- Mint leaves
- Ice cubes

RECIPE:

1. Add the apples to the juicer and extract the juice.
2. Add the grapes to the juicer and extract the juice.
3. Add them to a pitcher along with the orange juice and sparkling water. Mix until well combined.
4. Squeeze in the lemon juice and mix.
5. Chop the mint leaves and add to the pitcher.
6. Add in the ice cubes and mix until well combined.

GREEN APPLE SODA

INGREDIENTS:

- 1 cup green apple, chopped
- 1 cup plain soda
- 1 cup lemon juice
- ½ teaspoon salt
- 1 tablespoon honey
- Mint leaves
- Ice cubes

RECIPE:

1. Add the green apples to the juicer and extract the juice.
2. Add it to a pitcher along with the lemon juice and mix until well combined.
3. Add in the soda and mix well.
4. Add the salt and honey and combine.
5. Add the mint leaves and use a muddler to crush the mint leaves.
6. Add in the ice cubes and stir.
7. Serve cold.

GREEN APPLE LEMON JUICE

INGREDIENTS:

- 4 cup apples, chopped
- 1 cup orange juice
- 2 lemon, juiced
- Mint leaves
- Ice cubes

RECIPE:

1. Add the apples to the juicer and extract the juice.
2. Add them to a pitcher along with the orange juice and mix until well combined.
3. Squeeze in the lemon juice and mix.
4. Chop the mint leaves and add to the pitcher.
5. Add in the ice cubes and mix until well combined.
6. Serve cold.

APPLE HONEY GREEN TEA JUICE

INGREDIENTS:

For the Green Tea

- Combine 2 green tea bags with 4 cups of hot water and let it steep for 10 minutes. Remove tea bags and let it cool in fridge for 30 minutes

- 4 cups apples, chopped
- 1 cup pears, chopped

- ½ teaspoon salt
- 2 tablespoon honey (you can add more if you prefer it to be sweeter)
- Mint leaves
- Ice cubes

RECIPE:

1. Add the apples and pear to a juicer and extract the juice.
2. Combine the cooled green tea with the juice and mix well.
3. Add in the salt and honey and mix.
4. Add in the mint leaves and use a muddler to extract the flavor.
5. Add in ice cubes and mix.
6. Serve cold.

APPLE LIME MINT JUICE

INGREDIENTS:

- 2 cup apples, chopped
- 3 limes, juiced
- 1 cup white grape juice

- Mint leaves (you can be more generous for a minty taste)
- Ice cubes

RECIPE:

1. Add the apples to the juicer and extract the juice.
2. Combine the apple juice with the lime juice and grape juice, mix well.
3. Chop the mint leaves and add to the pitcher.
4. Add in the ice cubes and mix until well combined.
5. Serve cold.

Melon Your Coconuts

MELON AND PEAR SMOOTHIE

INGREDIENTS:

- 1 cup pear, chopped
- 1 cup watermelon, chopped
- 1 cup musk melon, chopped
- 1 large banana, chopped
- 2 cups plain yogurt
- ½ teaspoon salt
- 2 tablespoons sugar
- Mint leaves
- Ice cubes

RECIPE:

1. Add the pear, watermelon, muskmelon, banana and yogurt to a blender and whizz until well combined.
2. Add in the salt and sugar and whizz further.
3. Add the ice cubes and blend.
4. Serve cold with a sprinkling of mint leaves.

MELON AND COCONUT WATER

INGREDIENTS:

- 1 cup musk melon, chopped
- 1 cup coconut water
- 1 cup oranges, chopped
- ½ teaspoon salt
- 1 tablespoon honey
- Mint leaves
- Ice cubes

RECIPE:

1. Add the muskmelon to a juicer and extract the juice.
2. Add the oranges to a juicer and extract the juice.
3. Combine the two in a pitcher and mix until well combined.
4. Add in the salt and honey and mix well.
5. Add the mint leaves and use a muddler to crush it.
6. Add in ice cubes and mix well.
7. Serve cold.

MELON CARROT JUICE

INGREDIENTS:

- 1 cup carrots, chopped
- 1 cup melon, chopped
- 1 cup coconut water
- ½ teaspoon ginger, chopped
- ½ teaspoon salt
- 1 tablespoon honey
- 1 cup mint leaves
- Ice cubes

RECIPE:

1. Add the carrots to a blender and extract the juice.
2. Add the melon to a juicer and extract the juice.
3. Add both to a pitcher and mix until well combined.
4. Add in the ginger and mint leaves and crush to release flavor.
5. Add the salt and honey and mix until well combined.
6. Add in the ice cubes and stir.
7. Serve cold.

SPICY MELON JUICE

INGREDIENTS:

- 1 cup watermelon chopped
- 1 cup pineapple, chopped
- 1 cup lemon juice
- 1 green chili, deseeded
- ½ teaspoon salt
- 1 tablespoon honey
- Mint leaves
- Ice cubes

RECIPE:

1. Add the melon to a blender and whizz.
2. Add the pineapple to a juicer and extract the juice.
3. Add both to a pitcher and mix.
4. Toss in the lemon juice, chili, salt, honey and mix until well combined.
5. Add in the mint leaves and use a muddler to crush and release flavor.
6. Mix in the ice cubes.
7. Serve cold.

MELON PEACH JUICE

INGREDIENTS:

- 1 cup muskmelon, chopped
- 1 cup peach, chopped
- 1 cup orange juice
- ½ teaspoon salt
- 1 tablespoon honey
- Mint leaves
- Ice cubes

RECIPE:

1. Add the muskmelon to a juicer and extract the juice.
2. Add the peaches to a juicer and extract the juice.
3. Combine the two in a pitcher and mix well.
4. Add in the orange juice and mix until well combined.
5. Add the salt and honey and mix.
6. Add the chopped mint leaves and use a muddler to crush the leaves.
7. Add in ice cubes and mix until well combined.
8. Serve cold.

POMEGRANATE WITH COCONUT WATER

INGREDIENTS:

- 1 cup pomegranate, deseeded
- 1 cup coconut water
- 1 cup lemon juice
- ½ teaspoon salt
- 1 tablespoon honey
- Mint leaves
- Ice cubes

RECIPE:

1. Add the pomegranate to a juicer and extract the juice.
2. Add to a pitcher along with the coconut water and mix until well combined.
3. Add in the salt and mix.
4. Add the mint leaves and use a muddler to crush the leaves.
5. Add in the ice cubes and well combine.
6. Serve cold.

WATERMELON AND COCONUT WATER JUICE

INGREDIENTS:

- 1 cup watermelon, chopped
- 1 cup orange juice
- 1 cup coconut water
- ½ teaspoon salt
- Mint leaves
- Ice cubes

RECIPE:

1. Add the watermelon to the juicer and juice.
2. Add in the orange juice and blend until well combined.
3. Add to a pitcher along with the coconut water and stir until well combined.
4. Add in the salt and mix.
5. Add the chopped mint leaves and combine.
6. Toss in the ice cubes and mix well.
7. Serve cold.

ALOE VERA AND COCONUT JUICE

INGREDIENTS:

- 1 cup aloe vera, chopped
- 1 cup coconut water
- 1 cup lemon juice
- ½ teaspoon ginger, chopped
- ½ teaspoon salt
- 1 tablespoon honey
- 1 cup mint leaves
- Ice cubes

RECIPE:

1. Use a sharp knife to cut open an aloe vera leaf and remove the transparent sap from in between.
2. Add to a blender along with the coconut water and well combine.
3. Add to a pitcher along with the lemon juice, salt and honey and mix well.
4. Add in the ginger and use a muddler to crush and release flavor.
5. Add in the mint leaves and ice cubes and well combine.
6. Serve cold.

COCONUT SPINACH JUICE

INGREDIENTS:

- 5 cups spinach leaves, chopped
- 1 cup coconut water
- 1 cup lemon juice
- ½ teaspoon ginger, chopped
- ½ teaspoon salt
- 1 tablespoon honey
- 1 cup mint leaves
- Ice cubes

RECIPE:

1. Chop the spinach and add to a juicer to extract the juice.
2. Add to a pitcher along with the coconut water and lemon juice and mix until well combined.
3. Add in the ginger and mint and crush to release flavor.
4. Add the salt and honey and mix.
5. Add in the ice cubes and stir.
6. Serve cold.

COCONUT WATER AND GREEN GRAPES

INGREDIENTS:

- 2 cups coconut water
- 4 cups green grapes
- ½ teaspoon salt
- 2 tablespoons honey
- Mint leaves
- Ice cubes

RECIPE:

1. Add the grapes to a juicer and extract the juice.
2. Combine the juice with coconut water in a pitcher and mix well.
3. Add to a pitcher along with the salt and honey and mix until well combined.
4. Add in the ice cubes and mix.
5. You can also add in crushed ice.
6. Serve cold with a sprinkling of mint leaves on top.

Mangoes
Everywhere

MANGO GREEN TEA MILKSHAKE

INGREDIENTS:

- 1 cup mangoes, chopped
- 1 cup warm water, chopped
- 1 green tea bag
- 1 cup full cream milk
- 1 large banana, chopped
- 2 tablespoons sugar
- Mint leaves
- Ice cubes

RECIPE:

1. Add the warm water to a cup and place the green tea bag in it.
2. Allow it to steep for some time.
3. Meanwhile, add the mango, banana to a blender along with the cream and sugar and whizz until smooth.
4. Add in the tea and whizz further.
5. Add in the ice cubes and blend.
6. Serve cold with mint leaves on top.

MANGO MILKSHAKE

INGREDIENTS:

- 2 cups mango, chopped
- 2 cups full cream milk
- ½ teaspoon salt
- 2 tablespoons honey
- Mint leaves
- Ice cubes

RECIPE:

7. Add the mangos to a blender along with the milk and whizz until well combined.
8. Add to a pitcher along with the salt and honey and mix until well combined.
9. Add in the ice cubes and mix.
10. You can also add in crushed ice.
11. Serve cold with a sprinkling of mint leaves on top.

MANGO GREEN TEA MILKSHAKE

INGREDIENTS:

- 1 cup mangoes, chopped
- 1 cup warm water, chopped
- 1 green tea bag
- 1 cup full cream milk
- 1 large banana, chopped
- 2 tablespoons sugar
- Mint leaves
- Ice cubes

RECIPE:

7. Add the warm water to a cup and place the green tea bag in it.
8. Allow it to steep for some time.
9. Meanwhile, add the mango, banana to a blender along with the cream and sugar and whizz until smooth.
10. Add in the tea and whizz further.
11. Add in the ice cubes and blend.
12. Serve cold with mint leaves on top.

MANGO MILKSHAKE

INGREDIENTS:

- 2 cups mango, chopped
- 2 cups full cream milk
- ½ teaspoon salt
- 2 tablespoons honey
- Mint leaves
- Ice cubes

RECIPE:

12. Add the mangos to a blender along with the milk and whizz until well combined.
13. Add to a pitcher along with the salt and honey and mix until well combined.
14. Add in the ice cubes and mix.
15. You can also add in crushed ice.
16. Serve cold with a sprinkling of mint leaves on top.

MANGO PEACH SMOOTHIE

INGREDIENTS:

- 1 cup frozen mangoes
- 1 cup peaches, chopped
- 1 large banana, chopped
- 2 cups plain yogurt
- ½ teaspoon salt
- 2 tablespoons honey
- Mint leaves
- Ice cubes

RECIPE:

1. Add the peach and mangoes to a blender along with the banana and yogurt and whizz until smooth.
2. Add in the salt and honey and blend until well combined.
3. Toss in the ice cubes and blend.
4. Serve cold with a sprinkling of mint leaves on top.

MANGO AND CHILI JUICE

INGREDIENTS:

- 1 cup mangoes, chopped
- 2 red chilies, deseeded
- 1 cup lemon juice
- ½ teaspoon salt
- 1 tablespoon honey
- Mint leaves
- Ice cubes

RECIPE:

1. Add the mango to a blender and blend until well combined.
2. Add to a pitcher along with the lemon juice and mix until well combined.
3. Add in the chilies and use a muddler to crush.
4. Toss in the salt and honey and combine.
5. Add the mint leaves and mix well.
6. Add ice cubes and stir.
7. Serve cold.

Vegetable
Your Life

CARROT BEETROOT JUICE

INGREDIENTS:

- 1 cup carrots, chopped
- 1 cup beetroots, chopped
- 1 cup lemon juice
- ½ teaspoon ginger, chopped
- 1 cup mint leaves
- Ice cubes

RECIPE:

1. Add the carrots to the juicer and extract the juice.
2. Add the beetroots to the juicer and extract the juice.
3. Add both to a pitcher and mix until well combined.
4. Add in the lemon juice and mix until well combined.
5. Add in the ginger and use a muddler to crush and release flavor.
6. Add in the mint leaves and ice and mix until well combined.
7. Serve cold.

KALE AND CUCUMBER JUICE

INGREDIENTS:

- 1 cup kale leaves, chopped
- 1 cup cucumber, chopped
- 1 cup lemon juice
- ½ teaspoon ginger, chopped
- 1 tablespoon honey
- 1 cup mint leaves
- Ice cubes

RECIPE:

1. Add the kale leaves to a blender along with water and blend.
2. Add the cucumber to a juicer and extract the juice.
3. Add both to a pitcher and mix until well combined.
4. Add in the lemon juice and mix well.
5. Add the ginger and mint and use a muddler to extract the flavor.
6. Add in the ice cubes and mix.
7. Serve cold.

TAMARIND AND TOMATO JUICE

INGREDIENTS:

- 2 tablespoons tamarind pulp
- 1 cup tomatoes, chopped
- ½ teaspoon ginger, chopped
- ½ teaspoon salt
- 1 tablespoon sugar
- 1 cup mint leaves
- Ice cubes

RECIPE:

1. Add the tamarind pulp and tomato to a blender and mix until well combined.
2. Add in the ginger, salt, sugar and whizz until smooth.
3. Add to a glass along with the mint and crush.
4. Add ice cubes and serve cold.

BEETROOT POMEGRANATE JUICE

INGREDIENTS:

- 1 cup beetroot, chopped
- 1 cup coconut water
- 1 cup pomegranate, deseeded
- ½ teaspoon salt
- 1 tablespoon honey
- 1 cup mint leaves
- Ice cubes

RECIPE:

1. Add the beetroot to a juicer and extract the juice.
2. Add the pomegranate and extract the juice.
3. Combine both in a pitcher.
4. Add in the salt, honey and mix until well combined.
5. Add the ice cubes and mint and use a muddler to crush the leaves.
6. Serve cold.

SWEET POTATO AND CELERY JUICE

INGREDIENTS:

- 1 cup sweet potato, chopped
- 1 cup celery, chopped
- 1 cup lemon juice
- ½ teaspoon ginger, chopped
- ½ teaspoon salt
- 1 tablespoon honey
- 1 cup mint leaves
- Ice cubes

RECIPE:

1. Add the sweet potato to a juicer and extract the juice.
2. Add the celery, lemon juice, ginger, salt and honey to a blender and whizz.
3. Add both to a glass along with the potato juice and mix.
4. Add in the ice and serve with a sprinkling of mint leaves on top.

JUICE FOR HEALTHY SKIN

INGREDIENTS:

- 1 cup carrots, chopped
- 2 cups spinach leaves, chopped
- 1 cup apples, chopped
- 1 cucumber, chopped
- 1 teaspoon ginger, chopped
- ½ cup lemon juice
- Mint leaves
- Ice cubes

RECIPE:

1. Add the carrots to a juicer and extract the juice.
2. Add the spinach, apples, ginger and lemon juice to a blender and whizz.
3. Combine both in a glass along with the ice and mix.
4. Serve cold with a sprinkle of mint leaves.

TOMATO AND ORANGE JUICE

INGREDIENTS:

- 1 cup tomatoes, chopped
- 1 cup oranges, chopped
- 1 cup lemon juice
- ½ teaspoon ginger, chopped
- ½ teaspoon salt
- 1 tablespoon honey
- 1 cup mint leaves
- Ice cubes

RECIPE:

1. Add the tomatoes to a juicer and extract the juice.
2. Add the oranges to a juicer and extract the juice.
3. Add both to a pitcher and mix until well combined.
4. Add in the lemon juice and mix well.
5. Add the ginger and use a muddler to crush.
6. Add in the salt, honey and mint leaves and mix.
7. Add ice cubes and serve cold.

CELERY AND GARLIC JUICE

INGREDIENTS:

- 1 cup celery, chopped
- 1 cup coconut water
- 1 cup lemon juice
- ½ teaspoon garlic, chopped
- ½ teaspoon salt
- 1 tablespoon honey
- 1 cup mint leaves
- Ice cubes

RECIPE:

1. Add the celery to juicer and extract the juice.
2. Add it to a pitcher along with the coconut water and lemon juice and mix until well combined.
3. Add in the garlic and use a muddler to extract the flavor.
4. Add in the salt, honey and mint leaves and mix until well combined.
5. Add in the ice cubes and mix.
6. Serve cold.

BITTER GOURD AND LEMON JUICE

INGREDIENTS:

- 1 cup bitter gourd, chopped
- 1 cup cold water
- 1 cup lemon juice
- ½ teaspoon ginger, chopped
- ½ teaspoon salt
- 1 cup palm sugar
- 1 cup mint leaves
- Ice cubes

RECIPE:

1. Add the bitter gourd to a juicer and extract the juice.
2. Add to a pitcher and add in the lemon juice and mix until well combined.
3. Melt the palm sugar and add to the juice and mix.
4. Add in the salt and mint leaves and use a muddler to crush the leaves.
5. Add in the ice cubes and stir.
6. Serve cold.

BOTTLE GOURD AND GINGER JUICE

INGREDIENTS:

- 1 cup bottle gourd, chopped
- 1 cup pineapple juice
- 1 cup lemon juice
- 1 tablespoon ginger, chopped
- ½ teaspoon salt
- 1 tablespoon honey
- 1 cup mint leaves
- Ice cubes

RECIPE:

1. Add the bottle gourd to a juicer and extract the juice.
2. Add it to a pitcher along with the pineapple juice and lemon juice and mix until well combined.
3. Add in the ginger and mint leaves and use a muddler to crush and extract flavor.
4. Add in the salt, honey and ice cubes and mix until well combined.
5. Serve cold.

SWEET POTATO AND ORANGE JUICE

INGREDIENTS:

- 1 cup sweet potato, chopped
- 1 cup coconut water
- 1 cup oranges, chopped
- ½ teaspoon ginger, chopped
- ½ teaspoon salt
- 1 tablespoon honey
- 1 cup mint leaves
- Ice cubes

RECIPE:

1. Add the sweet potato to a juicer and extract the juice.
2. Add the orange to a juicer and extract the juice.
3. Add both to a pitcher and mix until well combined.
4. Add in the ginger and mint and crush.
5. Add in the salt, honey and mix until well combined.
6. Add in the ice cubes and mix.
7. Serve cold.

BELL PEPPER AND LEMON JUICE

INGREDIENTS:

- 1 cup green bell peppers, chopped
- 1 cup red bell peppers, chopped
- 1 cup lemon juice
- ½ teaspoon ginger, chopped
- ½ teaspoon salt
- 1 tablespoon honey
- 1 cup mint leaves
- Ice cubes

RECIPE:

1. Add the bell peppers to a juicer and extract the juice.
2. Add to a pitcher along with the lemon juice and mix well.
3. Add in the ginger and mint leaves and crush to release flavor.
4. Add the honey and salt and mix until well combined.
5. Add in ice cubes and serve cold.

CABBAGE AND MINT JUICES

INGREDIENTS:

- 1 cup cabbage leaves, chopped
- 1 cup mint leaves, chopped
- 1 cup lemon juice
- ½ teaspoon ginger, chopped
- ½ teaspoon salt
- 1 tablespoon honey
- 1 cup mint leaves
- Ice cubes

RECIPE:

1. Add the cabbage to a juicer and extract the juice.
2. Add in the lemon and mint to a blender and whizz until smooth.
3. Add both to a pitcher and combine.
4. Add in the ginger and mint leaves and crush.
5. Add honey and ice cubes and mix.
6. Serve cold.

CUCUMBER AND BROCCOLI JUICE

INGREDIENTS:

- 1 cup broccoli, chopped
- 1 cup cucumber, chopped
- 1 cup lemon juice
- ½ teaspoon ginger, chopped
- ½ teaspoon salt
- 1 tablespoon honey
- 1 cup mint leaves
- Ice cubes

RECIPE:

1. Add the broccoli to a juicer and extract the juice.
2. Add the cucumber to a juicer and extract the juice.
3. Add both to a pitcher along with the lemon juice and mix until well combined.
4. Add in the ginger, and mint leaves and crush to release flavor.
5. Add in the salt and ice cubes and mix well.
6. Serve cold.

PARSLEY JUICE

INGREDIENTS:

- 1 cup parsley leaves, chopped
- 1 cup coconut water
- 1 cup lemon juice
- ½ teaspoon ginger, chopped
- ½ teaspoon salt
- 1 tablespoon honey
- 1 cup mint leaves
- Ice cubes

RECIPE:

1. Add the parsley and coconut water to a blender and mix until well combined.
2. Strain into a pitcher and add in the lemon juice.
3. Mix well and add in the ginger and mint and crush.
4. Add the salt and honey and mix until well combined.
5. Add in the ice cubes and mix.
6. Serve cold.

RADISH AND LEMON JUICE

INGREDIENTS:

- 1 cup radish, chopped
- 1 cup cold water
- 1 cup lemon juice
- ½ cup lemon, cut into circles
- ½ teaspoon ginger, chopped
- ½ teaspoon salt
- 1 tablespoon honey
- 1 cup mint leaves
- Ice cubes

RECIPE:

1. Add the radish to a blender and extract the juice.
2. Add to a pitcher along with the lemon and mix until well combined.
3. Add in the ginger and crush.
4. Add the salt and honey and mix well.
5. Add in the mint leaves and ice cubes and stir.
6. Serve cold.

PEA AND ONION JUICE

INGREDIENTS:

- 1 cup green peas, boiled
- 1 cup white onion, chopped
- 1 cup water
- 1 cup lemon juice
- ½ cup palm sugar
- ½ teaspoon salt
- 1 cup mint leaves
- Ice cubes

RECIPE:

1. Add the boiled peas, onion and water to a blender and blend until well combined.
2. Add to a pitcher along with the lemon juice and mix well.
3. Add in melted palm sugar, salt and mint leaves and well combine.
4. Add in the ice cubes and mix.
5. Serve cold.

ASPARAGUS AND MINT JUICE

INGREDIENTS:

- 1 cup asparagus, chopped
- 1 cup lemon juice
- ½ teaspoon ginger, chopped
- ½ teaspoon salt
- 1 tablespoon honey
- 1 cup mint leaves
- Ice cubes

RECIPE:

1. Add the asparagus to a juicer and extract the juice.
2. Add to a pitcher along with the lemon juice and mix until well combined.
3. Add in the salt, honey and mix until well combined.
4. Add the ginger, mint leaves and ice cubes and mix well.
5. Serve cold.

ARTICHOKE AND LEMON JUICE

INGREDIENTS:

- 1 cup artichoke, chopped
- 1 cup cold water
- 1 cup lemon juice
- ½ teaspoon ginger, chopped
- ½ teaspoon salt
- 1 tablespoon honey
- 1 cup mint leaves
- Ice cubes

RECIPE:

1. Add the water and artichoke to a blender and whizz until smooth.
2. Strain and add to a pitcher along with the lemon juice and mix until well combined.
3. Add in the ginger and mint leaves and crush.
4. Add in salt, honey and ice cubes and stir.
5. Serve cold.

WATERCRESS AND CHILI JUICE

INGREDIENTS:

- 4 cups watercress, chopped
- 1 cup coconut water
- 1 cup lemon juice
- ½ teaspoon ginger, chopped
- 1 chili, deseeded and chopped
- ½ teaspoon salt
- 1 tablespoon honey
- 1 cup mint leaves
- Ice cubes

RECIPE:

1. Add the watercress to a juicer and extract the juice.
2. Add to a blender along with the coconut water and mix.
3. Add in the ginger and mint leaves and crush.
4. Add in the salt and honey and mix well.
5. Add in the ice cubes and stir.

BITTER GOURD AND CHILI DETOXIFIER

INGREDIENTS:

- 1 cup bitter gourd, chopped
- 1 cup coconut water
- 1 cup lemon juice
- ½ teaspoon ginger, chopped
- 2 red chilies, deseeded
- ½ teaspoon salt
- 1 tablespoon honey
- 1 cup mint leaves
- Ice cubes

RECIPE:

1. Add the bitter gourd to a blender and extract the juice.
2. Add to a pitcher along with the coconut water and mix until well combined.
3. Add in the lemon juice and mix.
4. Add the ginger and mint leaves and crush.
5. Add the salt and honey and combine.
6. Add ice cubes and serve cold.

PARSNIP AND LEMON JUICE

INGREDIENTS:

- 1 cup parsnip, chopped
- 1 cup coconut water
- 1 cup lemon juice
- ½ teaspoon ginger, chopped
- ½ teaspoon salt
- 1 tablespoon honey
- 1 cup mint leaves
- Ice cubes

RECIPE:

1. Add the parsnips and coconut water to a blender and extract the juice.
2. Add to a pitcher along with the lemon juice and mix until well combined.
3. Add in the ginger and mint leaves and crush.
4. Add salt, honey and ice cubes and mix well.
5. Serve cold.

EGGPLANT AND BEETROOT JUICE

INGREDIENTS:

- 1 cup eggplant, chopped
- 1 cup beetroots, chopped
- 1 cup lemon juice
- 1 tablespoon ginger, chopped
- ½ teaspoon salt
- 1 tablespoon honey
- 1 cup mint leaves
- Ice cubes

RECIPE:

1. Add the eggplant to a juicer and extract the juice.
2. Add the beetroot to a juicer and extract the juice.
3. Add both to a pitcher and mix until well combined.
4. Add the lemon juice and mix well.
5. Add in the ginger and mint and crush to release flavor.
6. Add the salt and ice cubes and mix.
7. Serve cold.

GRAPEFRUIT AND AVOCADO

INGREDIENTS:

- 1 cup grapefruit, chopped
- 1 cup avocado, chopped
- 1 cup lemon juice
- ½ teaspoon salt
- 1 tablespoon honey
- Mint leaves
- Ice cubes

RECIPE:

1. Add the grapefruit to a juicer and extract the juice.
2. Add in the avocado and lemon juice and whizz until well combined.
3. Add to a pitcher along with the grapefruit juice and mix until well combined.
4. Add in the salt and honey and mix.
5. Add the mint leaves and use a muddler to extract the flavor.
6. Add the ice cubes and mix.
7. Serve cold.

SUGAR CANE AND MINT JUICE

INGREDIENTS:

- 2 cups sugar cane, chopped
- 1 cup cold water
- 1 cup lemon juice
- ½ teaspoon salt
- 1 tablespoon honey
- 1 cup mint leaves
- Ice cubes

RECIPE:

1. Add the sugar cane to a juicer and extract the juice.
2. Add to a pitcher along with the water and lemon juice and mix until well combined.
3. Add in the salt and honey and mix well.
4. Add in the mint leaves and use a muddler to extract the flavor.
5. Add in the ice cubes and mix.
6. Serve cold.

TOMATO AND LEMONGRASS

INGREDIENTS:

- 1 cup tomatoes, chopped
- 1 cup lemongrass, chopped
- 1 cup lemon juice
- ½ teaspoon salt
- 1 tablespoon honey
- Mint leaves
- Ice cubes

RECIPE:

1. Add the tomatoes to a mixer and extract the juice.
2. Add the lemongrass and extract the juice.
3. Combine the two in a pitcher along with the lemon juice and mix until well combined.
4. Add in the salt and honey and mix until well combined.
5. Add in the chopped mint leaves and use a muddler to crush it.
6. Add in the ice cubes and stir.
7. Serve cold.

AVOCADO SMOOTHIE

INGREDIENTS:

- 2 cups avocados, chopped
- 1 large banana, chopped
- 2 cups plain yogurt
- ½ teaspoon salt
- 2 tablespoons sugar
- Mint leaves
- Ice cubes

RECIPE:

1. Add the avocados and banana to the blender along with the yogurt and whizz until smooth.
2. Add the salt and sugar and whizz further until smooth.
3. Add in the ice cubes and blend further.
4. Add to a glass and sprinkle with mint leaves on top.
5. Serve cold.

PUMPKIN SMOOTHIE

INGREDIENTS:

- 1 cup pumpkin, chopped
- 1 large banana, chopped
- 2 cups plain yogurt
- ½ teaspoon salt
- 2 tablespoons honey
- Mint leaves
- Ice cubes

RECIPE:

1. Add the pumpkin to a blender along with the banana and yogurt and whizz until smooth.
2. Add in the salt and honey and whizz further.
3. Add in the ice and crush until smooth.
4. Serve with a sprinkling of mint leaves on top.

CUCUMBER AND KALE SMOOTHIE

INGREDIENTS:

- 1 cup cucumbers, chopped
- 1 cup kale leaves, chopped
- 2 cups plain yogurt
- ½ teaspoon salt
- 2 tablespoons sugar
- Mint leaves
- Ice cubes

RECIPE:

1. Add the cucumbers and kale leaves to a blender along with the yogurt and whizz until smooth.
2. Add the salt and sugar and blend further.
3. Add the ice cubes and blend.
4. Serve with a sprinkling of mint leaves on top.

YAM SMOOTHIE

INGREDIENTS:

- 1 cup yam, chopped
- 2 cups plain yogurt
- ½ teaspoon salt
- 1 teaspoon ginger, minced
- 2 tablespoons sugar
- Mint leaves
- Ice cubes

RECIPE:

1. Add the yam to a blender along with the yogurt and whizz until smooth.
2. Add in the salt and sugar and whizz further.
3. Add the ice cubes and whizz.
4. Drop in the ginger and whizz.
5. Add to a glass along with the mint leaves and serve.

GINGER SMOOTHIE

INGREDIENTS:

- 1 cup avocado, chopped
- 1 cup kale leaves, chopped
- 1 cup parsley leaves, chopped
- 1 cup apples, chopped
- 1 tablespoon ginger, chopped
- 1/2 cup plain yogurt
- ½ teaspoon salt
- 2 tablespoons sugar
- Mint leaves
- Ice cubes

RECIPE:

1. Add the avocado, kale, parsley and apples to a blender along with the ginger and yogurt and whizz until smooth.
2. Add in the salt and sugar and whizz further.
3. Add the ice cubes and blend.
4. Serve cold with a sprinkling of mint leaves on top.

GINGER LEMON JUICE

INGREDIENTS:

- 1 cup lemons, cut into thin circles
- 1/2 cup ginger, chopped
- 2 cups lemon, chopped
- 1 cup cold water
- ½ teaspoon salt
- 1 tablespoon honey
- Mint leaves
- Ice cubes

RECIPE:

1. Add the lemons to the juicer and extract the juice.
2. Add to a pitcher along with the water and mix until well combined.
3. Add in the lemon slices and mix.
4. Add the ginger and use a muddler to crush gently.
5. Add the salt and honey and mix until well combined.
6. Add in chopped mint leaves and stir.
7. Add in ice cubes and serve cold.

ALL GREENS

INGREDIENTS:

- 1 cup green apples, chopped
- 1 cup pear, chopped
- 1 cup kiwi, chopped
- 1 cup avocado, chopped
- 1 cup lemon juice
- ½ teaspoon salt
- 1 tablespoon honey
- Mint leaves
- Ice cubes

RECIPE:

1. Add the apples, pear and kiwi to a juicer and extract the juice.
2. Add the avocado and lemon juice to a blender and mix.
3. Add both to a pitcher and mix until well combined.
4. Add in the salt, honey and mix.
5. Add the mint leaves and use a muddler to release flavor.
6. Add in the ice cubes and mix.
7. Serve cold.

SPINACH SMOOTHIE

INGREDIENTS:

- 5 cups spinach, chopped
- 2 cups plain yogurt
- ½ teaspoon salt
- 2 tablespoons honey
- Mint leaves, chopped
- Ice cubes

RECIPE:

1. Add the spinach leaves to a blender along with the yogurt and whizz until smooth.
2. Add in the salt and honey and whizz.
3. Add in the sugar and whizz.
4. Serve with a sprinkling of mint leaves on top.

PAPAYA GINGER JUICE

INGREDIENTS:

- 1 papaya, chopped
- ½ cup pineapple juice
- 2 tablespoons ginger
- ½ teaspoon salt
- 1 tablespoon honey
- 1 cup cold water
- Mint leaves
- Ice cubes

RECIPE:

1. Add the papaya to the blender along with the pineapple juice and whizz until well combined.
2. Add to the pitcher along with the ginger, salt and honey and use a muddler to crush the ginger.
3. Add in the cold water, mint leaves and ice and mix.
4. Serve cold.

CARROT PAPAYA MILKSHAKE

INGREDIENTS:

- 1 papaya, chopped
- 1 cup carrots, peeled and chopped
- 1 cups banana, chopped
- 1 cup almond milk
- ½ cup Greek yogurt
- 1 teaspoon vanilla extract
- Ice cubes

RECIPE:

1. Add the papaya, carrots and banana to a blender along with the almond milk and whizz until well combined.
2. Add in the Greek yogurt and whizz until smooth.
3. Add the vanilla extract and ice cubes and whizz, until ice is crushed and blended.
4. Serve cold.

Milkshake
The
Smoothie
Life

LYCHEE LASSI

INGREDIENTS:

- 2 cups lychee, chopped
- 1 cup plain yogurt
- ½ teaspoon salt
- 2 tablespoons white sugar
- 1 tablespoon fresh cream
- 1—2 cups ice cubes

RECIPE:

1. Add the lychee and yogurt to a blender and whizz until well combined.

2. Add in the salt and sugar and blend further.

3. Add the ice and whizz until smooth. You may need a little bit more if you prefer it to be thicker

4. Serve with a dollop of fresh cream on top.

LYCHEE PEACH SLUSH

INGREDIENTS:

- 2 cups lychee, chopped
- 2 cups frozen peaches
- 1 cup almond milk
- ½ cup Greek yogurt
- 1 tablespoon honey
- 2 cups ice cubes (to form a thick slush)

RECIPE:

1. Add lychee, peaches and almond milk to blender and whizz until well combined.

2. Add the Greek yogurt, honey and ice and whizz until it becomes a smooth, thick slush (you may need more ice)

3. Serve topped with lychee and mint leaves.

BANANA MILKSHAKE

INGREDIENTS:

- 2 cups banana, chopped
- 1/2 cup almonds, blanched
- 2 cups coconut milk
- ½ teaspoon salt
- 2 tablespoons honey
- Mint leaves
- Ice cubes

RECIPE:

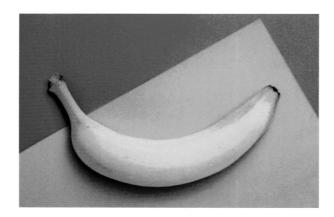

1. Add the bananas to a blender along with the almonds and coconut milk and whizz until smooth.

2. Add to a pitcher along with the salt and honey and mix it until well combined.

3. Add in the ice cubes and stir.

4. Serve cold with a sprinkling of mint leaves on top.

ORANGE AND ALMOND MILKSHAKE

INGREDIENTS:

- 1 cup orange, chopped
- 1 cup nectarines, chopped
- 2 cups almond milk
- 2 tablespoons honey
- Mint leaves
- Ice cubes

RECIPE:

1. Add the orange and nectarines to a blender and whizz until smooth.
2. Add in the almond milk and whizz.
3. Add to a pitcher along with the honey and mix until well combined.
4. Add in ice cubes and stir.
5. Serve with a sprinkling of mint leaves.

OREO MILKSHAKE

INGREDIENTS:

- 1 cup Oreo cookies, chopped
- 2 cups vanilla milk
- ½ teaspoon salt
- 2 Oreo cookies, crumbled
- Ice cubes

RECIPE:

1. Add the cookies to a blender along with the milk and salt and whizz until smooth.
2. Add in the ice cubes and crush.
3. Serve cold with crumbled Oreo cookies on top.

PINA COLADA SMOOTHIE

INGREDIENTS:

- 1 cups pineapple, chopped
- 2 cups coconut milk
- 1 cup coconut cream
- ½ teaspoon salt
- 2 tablespoons sugar
- Cherries, chopped
- Ice cubes

RECIPE:

1. Add the pineapple to a blender along with the coconut milk and whizz until smooth.

2. Add in the coconut cream and whizz.

3. Add in the salt and sugar until smooth.

4. Add in the ice cubes and whizz until blended.

5. Add to a cup and top with the cherries and extra slices of pineapple if desired.

6. Serve immediately.

RASPBERRY BUTTERMILK SMOOTHIE

INGREDIENTS:

- 2 cups fresh raspberries
- 1 cup frozen raspberries
- 1 cup plain yogurt
- About 1 cup plain buttermilk (you can use less, this adds to the creaminess of the smoothie)
- 1 tablespoon sugar
- ¼ cup Mint leaves and more for garnish
- Ice cubes

RECIPE:

1. Add the yogurt and buttermilk to a blender along with the raspberries and blend until well combined.
2. Add in the mint leaves and ice cubes and blend.
3. Serve with immediately with fresh mint leaves as garnish

SUMMER FRUIT SMOOTHIE

INGREDIENTS:

- 1 cup apples, chopped
- 1 cup blueberries
- 1 cup pineapple, chopped
- 1 cup papaya, chopped
- 1 cup musk melon, chopped
- 1 large banana, chopped
- 2 cups plain yogurt
- ½ teaspoon salt
- 2 tablespoons sugar
- Mint leaves
- Ice cubes

RECIPE:

1. Add the apples, blueberries pineapple, papaya, muskmelon and yogurt to a blender and whizz until smooth.
2. Add in the salt, sugar and blend until well combined.
3. Add in the ice cubes and whizz.
4. Serve cold with a sprinkling of mint on top.

PASSION FRUIT AND POMEGRANATE SMOOTHIE

INGREDIENTS:

- 1 cup passion fruit, chopped
- 1 cup pomegranate, deseeded
- 1 cup Greek yogurt
- 1 large banana, chopped
- 2 tablespoons sugar
- Mint leaves
- Ice cubes

RECIPE:

1. Add the passion fruit to a blender along with the pomegranate and banana and whizz.
2. Add in the yogurt and sugar and blend until smooth.
3. Toss in the ice cubes and whizz further.
4. Serve cold with a sprinkling of mint on top.

POMEGRANATE AND RASPBERRY MILK

INGREDIENTS:

- 2 cup pomegranate, deseeded
- 2 cups frozen raspberries
- 1 large banana, chopped
- 1 cup Greek yogurt
- 2 tablespoons honey
- 1 cup almond milk
- ½ cup ice cubes

RECIPE:

1. Add the pomegranate, raspberries and banana with the almond milk into the blender and whizz, until smooth.
2. Then add in the Greek yogurt, honey and ice cubes and blend until smooth.
3. The drink should resemble "milk" if it's on the thick side, you can add another ½ cup of almond milk.
4. Serve cold with frozen raspberries as your "ice cubes."

The Tea
Haven

TURMERIC TEA

INGREDIENTS:

- 1 inch cinnamon bark, grated
- 1 tablespoon turmeric powder
- 1 teaspoon clove
- 1 teaspoon nutmeg
- 1 tablespoon ginger
- 1 tablespoon black pepper
- 2 cups water
- 1 tablespoon honey
- 1 cup whole milk

RECIPE:

1. Add the cinnamon bark to a blender along with the turmeric, pepper, cloves, nutmeg and ginger and whizz to a powder.
2. Add in the water and honey and blend until smooth.
3. Add in the milk and blend until well combined.
4. Add the mix to a pan and bring to a boil.
5. Serve hot.

PARSLEY TEA

INGREDIENTS:

- 1 teaspoon cloves, crushed
- 1 large bunch parsley leaves, chopped
- 1 teaspoon ginger
- 1 teaspoon black pepper
- 2 cups of water
- 1 tablespoon honey
- 1 cup milk

RECIPE:

1. Add the parsley, cloves, ginger, and pepper to a blender and whizz until smooth.
2. Add in the water and honey along with the milk and combine.
3. Add the mix to a saucepan and bring to a boil.
4. Serve hot.

MINT TEA

INGREDIENTS:

- 1 large bunch mint leaves, chopped
- 1 tablespoon turmeric powder
- 1 teaspoon ginger
- 1 teaspoon black pepper
- 2 cups of water
- 1 tablespoon honey
- 1 cup milk

RECIPE:

1. Add the mint leaves, turmeric, ginger, pepper water to a blender and mix until smooth.
2. Add in the honey and milk and whizz further.
3. Add the mixture to a saucepan and bring to a boil.
4. Serve hot.

MINT AND POMEGRANATE TEA

INGREDIENTS:

- 1 teaspoon peppermints, crushed
- 1 cup pomegranate, deseeded
- 1 teaspoon ginger
- 1 teaspoon black pepper
- 2 cups of water
- 1 tablespoon honey

RECIPE:

1. Add 1-cup water to a saucepan and bring to a boil.
2. Add in the mint leaves and allow it to release flavor.
3. Add the ginger, pomegranate, pepper, water and honey to a blender and mix.
4. Add to a cup along with the strained mint tea and mix.
5. Serve hot.

ROSE PETAL TEA AND MELON

INGREDIENTS:

- 1 cup rose petals
- 1 cup melon, chopped
- 1 teaspoon ginger
- 1 teaspoon black pepper
- 1 cup of water
- 1 tablespoon honey

RECIPE:

1. Add one-cup water to a saucepan and toss in the rose petals.
2. Allow it to boil and release flavor.
3. Meanwhile, add the melon, ginger, pepper and honey to a blender and blend until smooth.
4. Add to a glass and mix in the strained rose water.
5. Serve hot.

HIBISCUS AND ROSE TEA

INGREDIENTS:

- ½ cup hibiscus flowers, chopped
- ½ cup rose petals, chopped
- 1 teaspoon black pepper
- 2 cups of water
- 1 tablespoon honey

RECIPE:

1. Add 1-cup water to a saucepan and bring to a boil.
2. Add in the hibiscus and rose petals and allow it to boil.
3. Meanwhile, add the pepper, water and honey to a blender and blend until well combined.
4. Add to a cup along with the strained tea and mix until well combined.
5. Serve hot.

LEMON AND MINT JUICE

INGREDIENTS:

- 1 tablespoon lemon juice
- 1 large bunch mint leaves, chopped
- 1 teaspoon ginger
- 1 green tea bag
- 1 teaspoon black pepper
- 2 cups of water
- 1 tablespoon honey

RECIPE:

1. Add 1-cup water to a saucepan along with the green tea and allow it to steep.
2. Add in the mint leaves to a blender along with the ginger, pepper and 1 cup water and honey and whizz until smooth.
3. Add in the lemon juice and tea and mix well.
4. Serve hot.

ROSEMARY TEA

INGREDIENTS:

- 1 cup rosemary leaves, chopped
- 1 teaspoon ginger
- 1 green tea bag
- 1 teaspoon black pepper
- 2 cups of water
- 1 tablespoon honey

RECIPE:

1. Add the water to a saucepan and bring to a boil.
2. Add in the ginger and green tea bag and allow it to steep.
3. Toss the rosemary leaves into a blender along with the pepper and 1 cup water and whizz.
4. Add to a cup along with the strained tea and mix.
5. Serve hot.

PEPPER AND TURMERIC TEA

INGREDIENTS:

- 1 teaspoon peppermints, crushed
- 1 tablespoon turmeric powder
- 1 teaspoon ginger
- 1 green tea bag
- 1 teaspoon black pepper
- 2 cups of water
- 1 tablespoon honey

RECIPE:

1. Add the tea bag to a 1-cup of boiling water.
2. Add the peppermint, turmeric, ginger, pepper and honey with 1 cup water and blend until well mixed.
3. Add to a cup along with the strained tea and serve hot.

GINGER AND RAW MANGO TEA

INGREDIENTS:

- 1 teaspoon raw mango powder
- 1 large bunch parsley leaves, chopped
- 1 teaspoon ginger
- 1 green tea bag
- 1 teaspoon black pepper
- 2 cups of water
- 1 tablespoon honey

RECIPE:

1. Add 1-cup water to saucepan and bring to a boil.
2. Add in the ginger and tea bag and allow to release flavor.
3. Meanwhile, add the mango powder, parsley leaves, pepper, 1 cup water and honey to a blender and whizz until smooth.
4. Add to a cup along with the strained tea and mix.
5. Serve hot.

CAYENNE PEPPER TEA

INGREDIENTS:

- 1 teaspoon cayenne pepper
- 1 large bunch mint leaves, chopped
- 1 teaspoon ginger
- 1 green tea bag
- 1 teaspoon black pepper
- 2 cups of water
- 1 tablespoon honey

RECIPE:

1. Add 1-cup water to a pan and bring to a boil.
2. Add in the tea bag and ginger and let it release flavor.
3. Add the cayenne pepper, mint leaves, 1-cup water and honey to a blender and whizz until smooth.
4. Add to a cup along with the strained tea and mix well.
5. Serve hot.

LEMONGRASS TEA

INGREDIENTS:

- 1 cup lemongrass, chopped
- 1 teaspoon ginger
- 1 teaspoon black pepper
- 2 cups of water
- 1 tablespoon honey

RECIPE:

1. Add 1-cup water to a saucepan and bring to a boil.
2. Add in the lemongrass and allow it to release flavor.
3. Meanwhile, add the ginger, water and honey to a blender and whizz until smooth.
4. Add to a cup along with the strained lemongrass tea and mix.
5. Serve hot.

THYME AND SAGE TEA

INGREDIENTS:

- 1 tablespoon thyme leaves, chopped
- 1 tablespoon sage leaves, chopped
- 1 teaspoon ginger
- 1 teaspoon black pepper
- 2 cups of water
- 1 tablespoon honey

RECIPE:

1. Add the water to a saucepan and toss in the thyme and sage leaves.
2. Allow them to come to a boil and release flavor.
3. Meanwhile, add the ginger, pepper, 1-cup water and honey to a blender and whizz.
4. Add this to a cup along with the strained thyme and sage tea and mix.
5. Serve hot.

CUMIN TEA

INGREDIENTS:

- 1 tablespoon cumin seeds, toasted
- 1 teaspoon ginger
- 1 green tea bag
- 1 teaspoon black pepper
- 2 cups of water
- 1 tablespoon honey

RECIPE:

1. Add 1-cup water to a saucepan and allow it to boil.
2. Toss in the tea bag and let it release flavor.
3. Add the cumin, ginger, water and honey to a blender and blend.
4. Add to a cup along with the strained tea and mix.
5. Serve hot.

BAY LEAF TEA

INGREDIENTS:

- 1 large bay leaf
- 1 teaspoon ginger
- 1 green tea bag
- 1 teaspoon black pepper
- 2 cups of water
- 1 tablespoon honey

RECIPE:

1. Add 1-cup water to a saucepan and bring to a boil.
2. Add in the bay leaf and tea bag and allow it to release flavor.
3. Meanwhile, add the ginger, pepper, water and honey to a blender and whizz until smooth.
4. Add to a cup along with the strained tea and mix.
5. Serve hot.

CORIANDER TEA

INGREDIENTS:

- 1 tablespoon coriander seeds, halved
- 1 large coriander leaves, chopped
- 1 teaspoon ginger
- 1 green tea bag
- 1 teaspoon black pepper
- 2 cups of water
- 1 tablespoon honey

RECIPE:

1. Add 1-cup water to a saucepan along with the tea bag and allow it to steep.
2. Add the coriander seeds, ginger, pepper, 1-cup water and honey to a blender and whizz.
3. Add to a cup along with the strained tea and mix.
4. Serve hot.

PEPPERMINT TEA

INGREDIENTS:

- 1 teaspoon peppermints, crushed
- 1 large bunch mint leaves, chopped
- 1 teaspoon ginger
- 1 green tea bag
- 1 teaspoon black pepper
- 2 cups of water
- 1 tablespoon honey

RECIPE:

1. Add the water to a saucepan and bring to a boil.
2. Add in the green tea bag and allow it to steep.
3. Meanwhile, add the ginger, peppermints, mint leaves, 1-cup water and honey to a blender and whizz until smooth.
4. Add to a cup along with the tea and mix until well combined.
5. Serve hot.

GINGER TEA

INGREDIENTS:

- 1 teaspoon cloves, crushed
- 1 tablespoon ginger
- 1 teaspoon black pepper
- 1 green tea bag
- 2 cups of water
- 1 tablespoon honey
- 1 cup milk

RECIPE:

1. Heat one-cup water and add to a cup along with the tea bag and allow it to steep.
2. Meanwhile, add the cloves, ginger, pepper and honey to a blender and whizz.
3. Add in the milk and whizz until well combined.
4. Add to a cup and mix in the tea.
5. Serve hot.

PEPPER AND TURMERIC TEA

INGREDIENTS:

- 1 teaspoon black pepper
- 1 teaspoon peppermints, crushed
- 1 tablespoon turmeric powder
- 1 teaspoon ginger
- 1 green tea bag
- 2 cups of water
- 1 tablespoon honey

RECIPE:

1. Add the tea bag to a 1-cup of boiling water.
2. Add the peppermint, turmeric, ginger, pepper and honey with 1 cup water and blend until well mixed.
3. Add to a cup along with the strained tea and serve hot.

TURMERIC HONEY MILK TEA

INGREDIENTS:

- 1 tablespoon turmeric powder
- 1 teaspoon ginger
- 1 Orange Pekoe tea bag
- 2 cups of boiling hot water
- 1 tablespoon honey
- 2 tablespoon cream

RECIPE:

1. Add the tea bag to a 1-cup of boiling water, let it steep while you prepare the other ingredients.
2. With the other 1 cup of boiling water, gently whisk in the turmeric powder and honey.
3. Combine the steeped tea and the dissolved turmeric and honey water in a large mug.
4. Add in the ginger and 2 tablespoons of cream, stir and serve hot.

Fruit For
Thought

Strawberry Basil Lemon

INGREDIENTS:

- 10 strawberries, sliced
- 1/2 lemon, sliced
- 5-10 leaves of fresh basil (depends on leaf size)

PREPARATION

1. In a large juice pitcher, layer the ingredients with cubes of ice.

2. Add fresh filtered water, and keep in fridge before serving.

Strawberry Mint and Raw Honey

Prep Time: 5 min

INGREDIENTS

- 10 strawberries, sliced
- 1/2 tablespoon Raw Honey dissolved in warm water (DO NOT use boiling water)
- 5-10 leaves of fresh mint (depends on leaf size)

PREPARATION

1. In a large juice pitcher fill it halfway with cubes of ice and fresh filtered water, and then stir in the Raw Honey water.

2. Add in the strawberry slices and mint and more cubes of ice and filtered water. Keep in fridge before serving.

Strawberry Pineapple Mint

INGREDIENTS

6 strawberries, sliced and 6 slices of pineapple (if using canned, make sure liquid is drained)

5-10 leaves of fresh basil (depends on leaf)

PREPARATION

1. In a large juice pitcher, layer the ingredients with cubes of ice.

2. Add fresh filtered water, and keep in fridge before serving.

Strawberry Cucumber Rose

INGREDIENTS

- 10 strawberries, sliced
- 6 cucumber slices
- 1/4 cup dried rose petals

PREPARATION

1. In a large juice pitcher, layer the ingredients with cubes of ice.

2. Add fresh filtered water, and keep in fridge before serving.

Strawberry Kiwi Lime

INGREDIENTS

- 10 strawberries, sliced
- 1 kiwi, peeled and sliced
- 1 small lime sliced

PREPARATION

1. In a large juice pitcher, layer the ingredients with cubes of ice.

2. Add fresh filtered water, and keep in fridge before serving.

Citrus Cucumber

INGREDIENTS

- 1/2 lemon cut into wedges
- 1 lime cut into wedges
- 10 slices of cucumber
- 5-10 fresh cilantro leaves (depends on leaf size)

PREPARATIONS

1. In a large juice pitcher, layer the ingredients with cubes of ice. Add fresh filtered water, and keep in fridge before serving.

Very Berry Cucumber

INGREDIENTS

- 1/2 cup fresh raspberries
- 1/2 cup frozen blackberries
- 6 cucumber slices

PREPARATIONS

1. In a large juice pitcher, layer the ingredients with cubes of ice. Add fresh filtered water, and keep in fridge before serving.

Orange Mint

IINGREDIENTS

- 1 large orange, cut into wedges
- 10 fresh mint leaves (depends on leaf size)

PREPARATION

1. In a large juice pitcher, layer the ingredients with cubes of ice.

2. Add fresh filtered water, and keep in fridge before serving.

Red Grapefruit and Rosemary

INGREDIENTS

- 1 grapefruit cut into wedges
- 2 sprigs of rosemary

PREPARATION

1. In a large juice pitcher, layer the ingredients with cubes of ice.

2. Add fresh filtered water, and keep in fridge before serving.

Grapefruit, Peach and Cucumber

INGREDIENTS

- 1/2 grapefruit cut into slices
- 1 small peach, peeled and sliced
- 6 cucumber slices

PREPARATION

1. In a large juice pitcher, layer the ingredients with cubes of ice.

2. Add fresh filtered water, and keep in fridge before serving.

Blueberry Lychee Mint

INGREDIENTS

- 1 cup blueberries
- 1 can of lychee, drained
- 5-10 leaves of fresh mint (depends on leaf size)

PREPARATION

1. In a large juice pitcher, layer the ingredients with cubes of ice. Add fresh filtered water, and keep in fridge before serving.

Blueberry Kiwi Lavender

INGREDIENTS

- 1 cup blueberries and 1 kiwi peeled and sliced
- 1 spring of dried lavender

PREPARATION

1. In a large juice pitcher, layer the ingredients with cubes of ice. Add fresh filtered water, and keep in fridge before serving.

Blueberry, Peach, and Lavender

INGREDIENTS

- 1 cup blueberries
- 1 white peach peeled and sliced
- 1 sprig of dried lavender
-

PREPARATION

1. In a large juice pitcher, layer the ingredients with cubes of ice. Add fresh filtered water, and keep in fridge before serving.

Blueberry Orange Mint

INGREDIENTS

- 1 cup blueberries
- 1 small orange, sliced
- 5-10 fresh mint leaves (depends on leaf size)

PREPARATION

1. In a large juice pitcher, layer the ingredients with cubes of ice. Add fresh filtered water, and keep in fridge before serving.

Lemon Ginger Raw Honey

INGREDIENTS

- 1 cup Raw Honey dissolved in some warm water
- 6 slices of ginger, washed and peeled
- 1 lemon, sliced

PREPARATION

1. In a large juice pitcher, layer the ingredients with cubes of ice.

2. Add fresh filtered water, and keep in fridge before serving.

Chrysanthemum and White Pear

INGREDIENTS

- 1 white pear, sliced
- 1 cup chrysanthemum dried flowers
- ½ cup Raw Honey dissolved in some warm water

PREPARATION

1. In a large juice pitcher, layer the ingredients with cubes of ice.

2. Add fresh filtered water, and keep in fridge before serving.

Rose Water with Pomegranate

INGREDIENTS

- 1 pomegranate, seeds removed, yield about 1 cup
- ½ cup dried rose petals

PREPARATION

1. In a large juice pitcher, layer the ingredients with cubes of ice.

2. Add fresh filtered water, and keep in fridge before serving.

The Power of Ginger

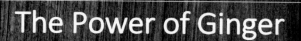

GINGER IS AN EXCELLENT INGREDIENT FOR BETTER DIGESTION, ESPECIALLY AFTER EATING OILY AND FRIED FOODS.

GINGER ALSO HELPS STIMULATE SALIVA, AND GASTRIC JUICE PRODUCTION TO AID IN DIGESTION. IT COULD ALSO HELP RELIEVE ANY BLOATING OR GASES TRAPPED IN YOUR DIGESTIVE SYSTEM.

Thank You

Thank you once again for choosing this book and hope you had a good time juicing through it!

The main aim of this book was to teach you the basics of the incorporating a juicing diet and provide simple recipes that you can try out at home.

Once you start with it, you will come face to face with its multiple benefits and turn it into a lifestyle choice.

HAPPY JUICING

74900950R00059

Made in the USA
Columbia, SC
08 August 2017